Published by: Experiments in Fiction

Text Design by: Ingrid Wilson

Cover Design by: Ingrid Wilson

ISBN: 978-1-7397577-0-0

Ingrid Wilson

40 POEMS AT 40

An
Experiments in Fiction
Publication

40 Poems At 40

INGRID WILSON

CONTENTS

Why 40 Poems At 40?

'They' say that 'life begins at 40,' and though I have scant idea who 'they' actually are, I do believe they might be onto something. I am publishing this short and highly personal poetry collection on the occasion of my 40th birthday as I feel in some way that this milestone marks a watershed: between the faltering and unsure steps of youth, through the years of self-doubt and even (at times) self-loathing, into a period of self-acceptance and quiet confidence. A period of reflection, serenity and gratitude balanced (as ever) with hard work.

'The child is father to the man,' wrote Wordsworth, and just as surely is the child mother to the woman. As a child, I wanted no more than to wander the mountains, writing my heartsongs. I lost sight of this pure joy in the spirit of creation as 'shades of the prison house' began to close upon me.

Work commitments, love and romance, and family life all came calling, not that I would for one moment call family life, or love, a 'prison house.' Work, yes. Addiction, yes. These things shut out the sunlight of the spirit long enough to stop me writing for over a decade. However, when my second son was born, this lit a fire within me. I was either going to become a Stepford wife, and live out the rest of my days in utter misery, or I was going to pursue my dreams with absolute conviction, and show my sons it can be done. I chose the latter path.

My poetry came back to me with sobriety. Once my head got clear, I became aware of the word-music that was constantly playing somewhere between my head and heart. I started to write some of it down. I shared it on 'Experiments in Fiction,' and the rest, as 'they' say, is history.

Isn't is a little egotistical...

...to write a book of poems with oneself as the main subject, a sketchy self-portrait adorning the front cover? I did wonder. The self-critical me would have told me not to even consider such a venture. But the self-loving me is learning, I have nothing to be ashamed of. I am sharing my experience, strength and hope with you, in the hope that something of it will speak to you, and perhaps give you renewed hope, or at the very least, a form of identification. I also hope that my words will give you pleasure. They should sound good to the ear, regardless of the meaning of the words. That is what I mean by word-music. And if you're coming to this book because you already know my work, and want to know a little more about me, some words of advice: read between the lines. These poems are not wholly autobiographical, nor are they all entirely about me. They trace the outline of a newly-emerging poetic consciousness.

Nevertheless, I am offering you a slice of my soul, for the price of a short book of poetry. I hope you find therein something of value.

— *I.W., December 2021*

For all the people who believe in me:
you know who you are
and I love you.

-       *I.W.*

1. Unexpected Things
A Villanelle

Life is full of unexpected things:
the clouds part to reveal a golden sky
as I breathe in the hope each new day brings.

Even in darkest winter, my heart sings
and I don't too much worry how, or why
this life is full of unexpected things.

A dream's a bird, which soars on open wings
lighting a flame within my memory
as I breathe in the hope each new day brings.

Caught off-guard where hidden passion flings
it's arms around me, fast-falling, I cry
that life is full of unexpected things.

Just as the rain-drenched magic whisperings
which passed secretly between you and I
so I breathe in the hope each new day brings.

And somehow that bold spark within me clings
to life, within the twinkling of an eye
wherein I find the hope each new day brings
for life is full of unexpected things.

2. The Mountains in Between

Further and further away from home
my travels took me, first
to Manchester's urban emptiness
to deep-dive into verse.

I sing the mountains in between
always returning to this first scene

Then to Newcastle, where I explored
the ruins of the ancient past
clues scratched in clay, as if to say,
'I lived here once, returned at last.'

I sing the mountains in between
always returning to this first scene

Then London's fields called out to me
a foundling on a jumbled sea
of multilayered history
bewitched, enchanted equally.

I sing the mountains in between
always returning to this first scene

Barcelona: beautiful horizon
drenched in Mediterranean sun
love lingers in her streets still
in my dreams I return.

I sing the mountains in between
always returning to this first scene

Malaga melting marble in
the mirage of a late-June afternoon
waking from the dream which almost killed me
none too soon.

I sing the mountains in between
always returning to this first scene

To dream into sobriety
inspired by some power, higher
breathing words of love to me:
rekindling a fire.

I sing the mountains in between
always returning to this first scene

Slovenia, od kod lepo te tvoje?*
Yet still I couldn't stay, for I'm
a stranger here and everywhere
though still I dare

to sing the mountains in between
always returning to this first scene

let me rest here.

*from whence derives your beauty?

3. One Poem at A Time

Can we change the world, one poem at a time?
The jury's out on this, however
never underestimate the power of the Word

it has endured millennia, for bad or good
according to its use
What to believe? It's up to you to choose:

this is not a polemical poem.

I've changed my life, one poem at a time:
in darkest times such words as soothed my soul
have healed me. In times of doubt, they have restored my
faith:

the power of a simple line of poetry
has brought about a fundamental change
in me, restoring inner light and harmony.

I'm not saying we can change the world,
but it's high time we tried our level best
so do your worst:

pick up a pen to write, a book to read, at least
to change your heart, at most
to change the rest.

4. The Freeze-thaw Weathering of My Heart

The freeze-thaw weathering of my heart
has been brutal.
Sometimes the freeze would last for months, or even years
at a time, but then
the thaw would come
melting into forgiveness
then just as suddenly would come the freeze again
so that large organ, expansive enough to contain whole
dimensions
would contract down
into the dense heart of a neutron star
shooting out pulsating beams of resentment
across the fabric of space-time
till it became
a paltry worn-out organ
barely battling to beat its own death march, imploding
into a black hole all its own
spaghettified, imagining
whole universes born.

5. Moondarkened

I spend the shadow-side
of my life in
Moondarkness
over on the far side of the moon
where no sound penetrates
we lose
radio contact
I pass in silent orbit
behind the shadows of everyday life
Moondarkened:
face to face with everything
I've ever hoped or feared;
Moondarkened
I'm a smoked-glass tinted
pain-inspired
seer.

My hope: to see you on the other side
My hope, you are still near.

6. Growing Through My Pain

I do believe I'm growing through my pain
though sometimes when the knife twists I still wince
I will not stoop to hate myself again.

Though sometimes when the knife twists I still wince
actions and words of others are their own
I've learned this, and I've practised ever since.

Actions and words of others are their own
as my own treasure house is my own soul
and knowing this, I face my fears alone.

As my own treasure house is my own soul
I have fought long, I have fought hard to keep it
and in self-keeping, still my dreams are whole.

I have fought long, I have fought hard to keep it
you cannot have it now, e'en if you would:
it's my reward, and only I shall reap it.

So as I take my leave of you, refrain
from telling me my pain has done no good:
I do believe I'm growing through my pain
I will not stoop to hate myself again.

7. Holding Up The Sky

I wake up tired from yesterday
spent holding up the sky;
there's seldom time to pause, or play
or ever wonder why.

I send the children off to school,
another laundry load
is done, while I feel like a fool
still struggling down the road

of holding up the sky each day
for each and everyone
who ever walks my weary way
afraid to walk alone.

And is that why I carry on
still holding up the sky
although my work is never done
perhaps until I die?

I only have myself to blame
when all is said and done
it's put up or it's shut up
until I put my foot down.

8. Wave Patterns

I have stood upon this shore so many times:

on the spring tide of 14
the summer swell of 21, the
neap tide of nearly 40

and the sea has told me many things:
the joy and power of love, of
fortunes won and lost

I've wanted a boat sometimes
and I'm not so strong a swimmer, but
the best is when you dive in

salt cakes your hair and skin
the cold sting takes your breath away
and gives you back your life

even when you go too far
and there's the fear you won't get back and
something else, detachedness — a strangeness

Thel is like a watry bow. and like a parting cloud.*
And what are we of any substance?
Wave patterns we leave behind on the sand

constantly weaving in and out this path of life
coming and going, waving goodbye, just
barely touching
everything.

(*Quote from The Book of Thel by William Blake, 1789-91)

9. Poem on Your Birthday

I remember
the coolness of your skin, and your warm heart
the thickness of your hair, and your thin body
seemed like the wind could blow right through you
which it did
it blows through me, too, though
it won't blow me over.

I remember
you waiting for me in the school yard
my favourite time of day
and the days you didn't come
the worst
and the one day you would never come again:
a nightmare.

Still, in time there are wild flowers again
and sunny days.
there is new life, new love
and still the old, which never left:
it's blowing in the wind
which blows through you
and blows through all things but cannot destroy
our love.

10. Some Scenes from My Life

A Cadralor

I.
Borrowdale rain sings
dancing on slate-grey rooftops
a rainbow paints the sky

II.
London's fields echo
with the sound of children playing
all the colours of joy

III.
Barcelona's patchwork streets
bewilder before welcoming
Trencadís enchantment

IV.
Malaga seethes
mirage upon marble
the sea softly sighs

V.
Clouds hang over Istria
stormwinds cry in chorus
where are you now?

11. Swift-like

Swift-like the way you broke my heart,
or like the way the kids grew up
the way you could down a pint, and I—a half,
or drain to the dregs a stained teacup.

Swift-like our lives which float on by
contrails in ever-changing sky.

12. Colours of November

A Cadralor

I.
Cold light at the bus station
spills into the port
crisps leaves to autumn gold

II.
Fairy lights in primary colours
fade to silver
fashions change

III.
Upon the slate-grey sea
the yearning waves
upend a tanker

IV.
Yellow for danger?
or simply a warning sign:
red is for danger

V.
All the colours of my heart
blend into this November light
windblown, standing, still.

13. We are not Alpha nor Omega neither

We are not alpha nor omega neither, rather
somewhere on that universal spectrum we can barely
understand:
we've done our maths, and claim to know the ratio of all
things
except the things we don't, which we call 'dark'
(we used to call them 'God')
but now

we've made gods of ourselves, reasonable creatures, and
the measure
of all rational achievement, progress
towards power to destroy ourselves
and all who abide with us
as we cry out 'Hallelujah!' 'Men of reason, men of science'
always men,
from the Big Beard in the sky on down
to all his henchmen here on Earth.

Rebirth
is taking time outside of time, just to
become aware that we contain whole universes, just as
whole universes contain us
misunderstood continuum, this
disc with only one side
wonder, wonder
only one another
holding one, another

World Without End.

14. Cadralor No.3

I.
Moth on the windowpane
buzzing, busy wings
blindly fumbling

II.
Stars hang in constellation
measuring the depths of
astronomical time

III.
A home fire burns
in the warm hearth
down to ash

IV.
Sweets from a jar
prizes for the children
rainbow coloured

V.
Sticky-handed, I
am a child again:
the universe, within

15. Poem for My Children

Let not my words die with me
after all is said and done
I dedicate these words to you,
continue on alone.

Let not my words die with me
at the closing of my day:
they're all I ever had to give
and now I cannot stay.

Let not my words die with me,
let them linger in the light
of eventide, e'en as I fade
into the darkling night.

Let not my words die with me
and I cannot be afraid
that I am leaving you alone
with too much left unsaid.

But let my words live with you
let them echo down the years,
let them resound and comfort you
when I'm no longer near.

Yes, let my words live with you
as your true inheritance
and all I ever had to give:
love and remembrance.

16. Feeding The Ducks at Bohinj

All day long, rain:
falling from the low cloud,
falling foul of my low mood,
falling.

Visibility down to ten percent:
light aircraft grounded for today
and far away
somewhere in a far-off land
I'd left behind
sunshine.

Rain like my tears
which I refused to let fall:
let the sky fall tears for me,
fall like an edgeless sword
courting despair.

Where had the sun gone?
When would he be back again?
friends told me happily
perhaps even a little smugly that
he shone on England.

All day long, rain
all day with no change
what to do
with two un-tired and restless
children?

'Shall we feed the ducks?'
I said,
'Oh yes, oh yes, let's go!' they cried:
'Let's go to Bohinj.'

On the drive
clouds swirled
much better than low mizzle
sweeping, swirling low across
the theatre of the sky:
promising drama.

At the shore
the campsite full of life
like adolescent memories of
happy hikers huddled
underneath the wooden canopy
all drinking, laughing, living,
being merry.

At the water's edge
the children threw out bread
to lure the far-away ducks
and we watched as they approached
all unperturbed
by thunder.

Heavy raindrops
fresh-fallen tears now
from the heavy sky
are dropping pebble-like
into the lake

Joy:
joy on the faces of the children
joy at childhood memories of
innocence revived
joy in campsite conviviality
joy in the sunburst which would follow
washing the leaves a fresh, redolent
green.

17. Can We Steal Away?

I should have been writing
glued to my desk in darkness but
the Sun called
just to say

'Can we steal away now:
over the mountains
I'll lead you
and nothing more you'll have to do
than follow your heart's desire
say, wouldn't you just love to?'

And what was I to do:
I, who am so much a fool
for winter sunlight
that I'll brave the cold all day for it?
Defrosting myself now
writing this message
just to say:
'Dear Sun-across-the-hills,
I'm glad I chose to steal away
with you.'

18. Nature Paints A Picture in Her Beauty
A Pantoum

Nature paints a picture in her beauty
which we can only imitate in art
nor can we match her bright majestic glory
with painted brushstrokes or the lines we write:

So we can only imitate in art
a paltry shadow of nature's creation
with painted brushstrokes or the lines we write
we seek to match our natural fascination.

A paltry shadow of nature's creation
is all we can accomplish for our pains
we seek to match our natural fascination
but end up wishing for material gains.

Is all we can accomplish for our pains
a little limelight, wealth, or even fame?
We end up wishing for material gains
and lose the spark once lit by nature's flame:

Our little limelight, wealth, or even fame
can never match that bright majestic glory
we lose the spark once lit by Nature's flame
as Nature paints a picture in her beauty.

19. Sava Bohinjka
An Extended Sonnet

Your crystal waters plummet from their source
at Slap Savica: powerful, rainbow-painting
here at the origin, you find your voice
and down into the valley, let it sing

silently, reflectively at first
in limpid pools and under boulders, whisper
secrets to serenely sleeping Earth
and those who would disturb her quiet slumber

not out of ignorance, to aggravate
but hoping to hear secrets for themselves
they stop a while, and watch, and patient wait
while gentle winds set down the dying leaves

thus in this season of encroaching death
we seek the light reflected in your mirror
secrets of youth: the spark, the dance, a breath;
the sacred wisdom of the silent river.

20. The Snow Queen

The first snow of winter has fallen, The
Snow Queen has lain her cloak upon the ground:

Be careful not to catch a snowflake in your heart

for though they may be beautiful, their crystals contain
slivers of glass from the dark enchanted mirror
dropped to Earth moments before The Fall
and if you catch that snowflake in your heart, all
will be darkness and despair within you,
which will emanate, to freeze in turn
the hearts of those close by
just as the Snow Queen lays her freezing cloak
upon the ground; don't say I didn't warn you:

Be careful not to catch a snowflake in your heart.

21. Solstice of The Heart

The darkest day is done at last
yet I'm not past
the solstice of the heart;

when all you thought was solid
slips like sand beneath your feet
some say it is the dark night of the soul,
but I call it the solstice of the heart:

When friends and lovers slip away
The solstice of the heart
When nothing good, or gold, can stay
The solstice of the heart

Perhaps it is the way our faith is tested, if
we can dance on a Friday
when the sky turns black, perhaps
we will turn back
toward the light, toward
that distant beacon,
dazzling: summer
solstice of the heart.

22. Dancing Ice Queen

You come to look for a king
why him?
Will he melt the ice around your heart
if you play your part

right? Will you find sweet
delight, gliding across the ice
fingers frozen
heart alight?

Light is but a dream
(it's all there is)
but all's not as it seems
your breath peals out as mist

the scene fades at the seams:
Dancing Ice Queen
not so young and sweet
as you once were, but sweeter

'tis to know yourself
and melt the ice-shard at your core
in knowing what you always were
though unaware before.

23. Points North

Wheels in motion and the wind
whips around behind my ears
at the nape of my neck
in a subtle caress
and I know I'm being propelled

along a river of life
whose course and motion
I do not pretend to understand
sometimes I like it when the waters
speed me down towards a sea
sunless and sighing

till the cloud breaks
and I see
the sky is crying
and at sundown
out come all the thousand stars
and I can name the constellations

in this hemisphere
at any time of year
there is always the Plough
above, or the Big Dipper
and at its tip, Polaris
The Pole Star
Points North.

And so I have my fixed
celestial compass
though I do not
always understand the path
or the trajectory
I know well my own
portion of the sky,
the earth below, above only the heavens and
Points North.

24. Points South

I've heard there is a Southern Cross
that's seen in the Antipodes at night:
I've never seen the Southern Hemisphere
nor the *Aurora Australis*
— I'm sure it's a delight.

Some people say
Points South
are what's between the legs,
below the mouth
but I've heard that
The Southern Cross also
points South:

I'd be lost in The Outback
unless an aboriginal guide
equipped with ancient wisdom
could help out
a sunburnt squinting and bewildered
stranger; sharing
all the secrets of the scorched earth and
Points South.

25. A Sailor of Sorts

I've always felt at home upon the sea
more so than on land
even in a storm
much more like life to me
the roaring waves
beyond the shifting sand:

A wilderness unbound by borders
here where all lands end;
here where there be
dragons, regions uncharted, and
beyond it all, below — the Underworld.

Past Scylla and Charybdis I have sailed
on into the Bermuda Triangle
my trim was off, mists grew
my compass failed
but still I made it through all-but unscathed.

Tsunamis I have surfed, but none so harsh
as they could drown me;
I was made for this
like many a woman before me
whose fate was sealed: to stand, to wait and wish.

For creatures of ill-omen women we
were once believed
by mariners to be, or
lusty sirens luring them
to sleep eternal deep beneath the sea

but I don't fear opinions of men,
or anyone
who would keep me ashore
I've built a boat that's all my own;
with sails for wings I'll soar.

And when the sea is calm I'll know
I've circumnavigated life
the cycle turned
full circle, brings me surely, brings me safe
if not to harbour, then at least to peaceful waters, freed
from strife.

26. Anchor/Safe Harbour

Looking for a hook on which to hang my hopes
expectantly, I hung my hopes on you;
looking for a spot on which to fix my dreams
fixatedly, I obsessed over you:

'What can I do, I'm falling?'
My refrain:
'Let everything fall down
for I'm in love.'

Looking for a place to call my own
I told myself I'd found that place in you;
looking for a space which never was my home
I told myself my home was here with you:

And when it all fell down
what was the answer?
To weep and cry? To moan
and gnash my teeth?

Looking for an anchor in a troubled life
times when I could not see the way to shore
I found safe harbour through my deepest strife:
The answer lies within; I'll seek outside no more.

27. You and Me, Sea
A Love Song

Ain't it just like you and me, Sea
when we dance together,
I barefoot on the sand, you
lapping at my toes?

Ain't it just like we're two parts of
the same whole:
I was born of you, and you
bring me to life once more?

Ain't it just like you and me, Sea?
and we've always been together
dancing a saline tango in the sun.

Ain't it just like you and me, Sea?
When I hit stormy weather
on your shore I'll wind up, by the wild winds
flung.

Say, it's just like you and me, Sea;
I can hear you calling:
your echo fills my silent afternoon.

And that was all I wanted to say, Sea:
When I'm far away from you
I feel your surge in me which swells into
a tide to take me home.

28. She's Let Herself Go

She's let herself go:
two children
almost 50 years
love and heartache
lines etched in her face
can't be erased now:
she has let herself go.

She's let herself go:
too many gold hairs turned to grey
has she not heard of hair dye?
Looks as though the answer's 'no,'
I say, I say
she's surely let herself go.

She's let herself go:
is Botox too expensive?
Some women her age really take care of themselves
and still look quite attractive
but as for her, well
she has let herself go.

She's let herself go
to the dogs
perhaps it's nature's way:
she's no longer a viable vessel
so why not let herself go
when she's no longer of
procreational value anyway?

She's let herself go:
far too many chocolate bars
those comfort foods go straight onto her hips.
She never should have let such sweetness pass her lips;
she tries to run, but trips:
she's let herself go.

She's let herself go
down to the beach today
all alone,
no one to bar her way
and topless she dances as the sun kisses
her sunken breasts
which have nourished two children

she's let herself go
exactly where she needs to go,
nobody's vessel and instead
a Goddess, yes!
So let them all say, 'she has let herself go'
and she'll tell them all where they can go:
the place, I think you'll guess.

29. Like Laurel Canyon Carole King

Right now, I'd love to live
like Laurel Canyon Carole King
the beehives and false lashes
replaced by wilder tresses
not locked in the Brill Building
writing songs
for other folks to sing
not having to wipe the baby's ass
with pen in one hand
diaper in the other
writing a song for an old friend
or a brother:
Just like Laurel Canyon Carole King
a *Natural Woman*
happy and free
wheelin', and
feelin' *Beautiful –*
Some Kinda Wonderful
in my own skin.

30. The Freedom of The City

I walk the streets once more and feel
the freedom of the city
after being absent for so long
freedom of
sweltering summer heat
sweating in the shade and
aching swollen feet
freedom of anonymity
freedom of all life in one day
freedom of history mingled with modernity
freedom is salty sweat-tang
freedom is sunlit street
freedom is the rhythm of
human life, imperfect
yet perfect
for today
I feel
the freedom of the city.

31. The Lullaby of Venice

The moon is hung midway in the sky;
it lights on the water
where cradled am I;
gondola-rocked in my lullaby:
The Lullaby of Venice.

The footsteps of tourists have fallen away
as they all tend to do at the end of the day
to their hostels and hotels they've wended their way
with nary a cry, only
The Lullaby of Venice

Throw open the shutter and hear the canal
as it slaps on the slab-stones and wishes you well
in the lamplight the Ivy hangs down so to tell
one sweet wish to the well like
The Lullaby of Venice

And this beautiful city, this glittering jewel
is backsliding, subsiding into the lagoon
and I hope it won't be drowned, and over too soon
by the light of the moon, the lost
Lullaby of Venice

32. Trafalgar Square Triptych

I.
It's summertime in Trafalgar Square;
we've stopped to feed the pigeons there:
It must be early on in the World Cup
because my young son sports an England top
still holding out a hope
(We went out in the first round that year.)

II.
Still it's summertime 20 years earlier
Trafalgar Square is there, as ever
I'm sporting an injury — black eye from
downhill biking without breaks.
My mother's not been dead two years:
unhealed wounds walk with me.

III.
Fast-forward to when wintertime
has made it to Trafalgar Square
my sister's not been dead two weeks
and I'm trying to negotiate the
Christmas shopping crowds as
iced winds rip right through me.

33. In London

Returning to London after 5 years
not the passing, but the standstill of time
hits like a double-decker bus
up front and personal
the past is present
everywhere.

What's past is prologue
Christmas lights adorn Trafalgar Square:
where are you now?
Where were you then?
Already gone, too soon
sister Alison.

The sparkle and glitter of the gaudy baubles
did not warm but chilled my heart
as you lay in a hospital bed
I had to get back
and hold your hand
but could not bring you back.

Now, I hold my children's hands
and feel the warmth return
to my heart, and the light
to my eyes, just
as it once shone in yours,
now shines in theirs.

34. My Father's Garden

My father's garden is overgrown,
a jungle of wild flowers from
my mother's time.

She loved the wilderness, transplanted it.
It bloomed because of her
green-fingered magic.

I feel it still:
my favourites are the peonies which bloom
each June, ephemeral
brightest of all.

35. Swimming with Sharks

Been swimming with sharks
all my life, so it seems
started before I saw 'Jaws,' started
in the playground
girls with pearl-white smiles, knee socks and
patent-leather shoes
pretending friendship
waiting to bite, turn you out
into the sea of isolation.

Been swimming with sharks all my life
did I mention? The men, too, had their smiles
couldn't wait to sink their teeth
into young flesh
so it was then. So I was
foolish fish, but never destined
to become someone else's dish.

Been swimming with sharks all my life
in the workplace
where they went by the name
of 'manager,' 'supervisor,' anything
to give them a little power
over anyone
remotely unshark-like
like me.

Been swimming with sharks all my life
and those shades in the sea
who have been here much longer than us:
I do wonder, why not let them be?
But you can't, can you?
Because you just can't see

that the most bloodthirsty shark of all
is the shark in your psyche
twisted by too many turns in
a too-shallow sea
that's called life, and sure, as it swims within you
I can promise,
it swims within me.

36. In Too Few Words...

Perhaps I use too few words
in my poetry,
I don't tend to favour over-long words,
that have me reaching for the dictionary.

There's a skill and wit in brevity,
in the crafting of a message directly
in such a way that it can be
remembered easily,

e.g.,

In too few words
you say the things that hurt the most:
'I'm leaving.'
'It is over.'
'It was never really love.'

In too few words, I say the opposite
to try and hold you close:
'I love you.'
'Don't leave me.'
'Think it over one more time.'

And when I think it over
there were too few words
of love for me there
(always my mistake.)

This time

I think I'll take
a new perspective:
sit down at my writing-desk and
change the aspect ratio, try to distil
the yearnings of the heart
into few words.

37. Reclusive Romance

What do you know of me?
I've been up for hours whilst you lay sleeping.
I've heard the wind whisper, and the moon sing
Don't tell me you know me.

What do you think of me?
Little, if anything:
mind my own business, am always in hiding.
Don't think you can know me.

What do you want of me?
What is so interesting?
Do you find watching my life so amusing?
I want you to leave me.

What do I know of you?
Always interior, looking within,
and so I admit with a smile and a grin that
I know nothing of you.

What do I think of you?
You're really quite handsome, from what I have seen:
your eyes are like diamonds, your smile is serene…
I don't often think of you.

What do I want of you?
Hard to explain it, where to begin?
I couldn't support ever letting you in
but the truth is, *I want you.*

38. Unsung

I am the song unsung,
the life unlived,
the word as yet unwritten:
I ground the grain to make your bread
while you conquer'd empires
and dreams
and concubines
and while you drank the red, sweet wine of youth
I aged at home.

I'm Shakespeare's sister, the
madwoman in the Attic and
the Angel in the House, as yet unkilled.
So write, you bards and balladeers,
write your immortal lines
and praise me with your elegiac verse
(I'll be your muse
and bind my words in dreams)
but yet be warned:

I want the words you stole from me,
the life I gave,
the song as yet unsung.
As once upon a time the High Priestess
processioning, skirts rustling to grace
the altar with a knife held high
was heard
I've found my voice
whose blade
cuts out your tongue:
Now hear my song.

39. I Do Not Know My Mother's Name

I do not know my mother's name: she got it from her father,
and her mother, from her father before her.
Our herstory has been erased
by history,
records always follow the paternal line.

Matrilineal DNA might help,
if we had all the samples
but most of them lie
a long-time underground
(or burnt to ash).

We silently accepted
an unspoken, acknowledged misogyny
and had our story stolen
time after time
tacitly complicit
in our own self-erasure:

I took his name
but you will know of mine.

40. Queen of The Last Line

Queen of the last line
of defence, I stake
an arrow through your heart
most cupid-like
and wait for you to feel it.

Direct hit: you are falling
under my powerful spell
it may lead you to heaven
or drag you down to hell:
don't say you didn't want it.

Queen of the last line
drawing a circle around you,
and drawing you in:
there's no easy way out
(I feel you should know this
before you begin.)

I've done my due diligence:
you, I'm determined to know
and in return you will come
to think you know me,
though rest assured
it isn't so.

Queen of the last line
I'll take my sweet time
as I draw you in again,
then cast you out.
If you planned to become mine
you were deceived by your every last
thought.

Queen of the last line
of defence, I stake
an arrow through your heart
and though you try to pull it out
you'll never fail to feel it.

Made in United States
North Haven, CT
25 April 2022

18556546R00050